Vanilla

Vanilla

Over 50 sublime vanilla-flavored recipes

hamlyn

Notes

The American Egg Board advises that eggs should not be consumed raw. This book contains some dishes made with raw or lightly cooked eggs. It is prudent for more vulnerable people such as pregnant and nursing mothers, invalids, the elderly, babies, and young children to avoid uncooked or lightly cooked dishes made with eggs.

This book includes dishes made with nuts and nut derivatives. It is advisable for those with known allergic reactions to nuts and nut derivatives and those who may potentially be vulnerable to these allergies, such as pregnant and nursing mothers, invalids, the elderly, babies, and children, to avoid dishes made with nuts and nut oils. It is also prudent to check the labels of pre-prepared ingredients for the possible inclusion of nut derivatives.

First published in Great Britain in 2005 by Hamlyn,
a division of Octopus Publishing Group Ltd,
2–4 Heron Quays, London E14 4JP

Copyright © Octopus Publishing Group Ltd 2005

ISBN 0 600 61350 X
EAN 9780600613503

A CIP catalog record for this book is available from the British Library

Printed and bound in China
10 9 8 7 6 5 4 3 2

Contents

Introduction

A familiar flavor

We're all familiar with the flavor and aroma of vanilla, which is used in many everyday products, both food and non-food. However, its unique traits are often artificially copied, because the cost of genuine vanilla means it must be saved for special occasions. The time and energy that have to be invested in the plants in order to produce the beans or pods more than justify the fact that vanilla is one of the world's most expensive spices. However, nothing quite compares to the flavor of real vanilla beans or vanilla extract, and once you've become accustomed to the many uses of this unique spice, you will probably start to include it in an increasing number of recipes. With such a

Vanilla is the fruit of a tropical orchid called Vanilla fragrans.

wonderful history surrounding it and the time and effort involved in its production and preparation for culinary use, it's no wonder that vanilla is regarded so highly. Its sweet, aromatic flavor has enthralled people for many hundreds of years and you're sure to fall under its spell as soon as you've tried your first vanilla recipe.

Living legend Although there is little historical documentation about the ways in which vanilla was originally used, legend has it that the Totanec people of Mexico were cultivating the plant 1,000 years ago, its emergence coinciding with the death of a beautiful princess, Tzacopontziza. It was believed that the aromatic plant was her spirit living on among the people. It is still cultivated and revered by the Totanec people today. It wasn't until 1518, however, that the first written references to vanilla were recorded. That was the year in which Hernando Cortés, the Spanish conquistador, came across *chocotatl*, a luxurious drink of cocoa infused with vanilla, which was enjoyed by the emperor and other dignitaries. This was considered such an important find that both these ingredients were given pride of place among the riches that Cortés took when he left to return to Spain. It didn't take long for vanilla to become popular throughout Europe as people developed a taste for the exotic spices of the New World.

Flower power Many people are surprised to learn that vanilla is actually the fruit of a tropical orchid, *Vanilla fragrans*. About 150 varieties are grown around the world, but only two, 'Bourbon' and 'Tahitian,' are used commercially. The species is native to Mexico, and for many years this was the only country where the plant would grow. After its discovery by Europeans, numerous attempts were made to grow it and cultivate the beans elsewhere, but the plant refused to bear fruit. The reasons for the failure confounded botanists for years until it was eventually discovered that a small bee, native to Mexico, was the only insect that could pollinate the seeds. Techniques of hand-pollination were eventually developed, and the plant is now successfully grown in other countries.

Labor of love Today, Indonesia and Madagascar are the world's leading producers of vanilla, with a number of countries in Central America and the Caribbean also growing the crop. Vanilla is also produced in China and India. It is said to be the most labor-intensive cultivated crop in the world to grow, no doubt partly due to the fact that it takes three years before the plant starts producing any fruit and a further nine months before the beans can be harvested. After harvesting, the beans have to be left to cure so that the distinctive flavor and aroma develop fully. This usually involves laying them out to dry under the sun and covering them at night, and repeating this a number of times until they start to resemble the beans that we see in stores.

Vanilla variations

There can be quite significant differences in flavor between vanilla beans grown within relatively short distances, and, obviously, as the distance grows, so the flavors become even more diverse. It takes a connoisseur to be able to discern the characteristics of different vanilla crops, but we should perhaps be aware that there are subtle nuances that might affect the overall flavor of a dish.

In spite of the regional differences, there are certain characteristics that should be present in all good-quality vanilla beans. The most important is the aroma, which should be completely distinctive, indicating that the beans have been cured sufficiently. The pods themselves should feel slightly oily when you touch them. If they are dry and crumble easily in your hands, they are of poor quality and you should avoid using them.

Storing vanilla

Despite the time and effort involved in their production and their delicate nature, vanilla beans are remarkably tough when it comes to culinary use. Although it may seem expensive compared to other flavorings—and to cheaper vanilla imitations—it's well worth spending the extra money on the real thing. If they are treated correctly, vanilla beans can be used time and again for many types of flavoring, so don't discard used beans. The flavor and aroma are contained throughout the outer pod, as well as in the seeds, so if you're using whole beans to flavor milk, custards, and sauces, you can simply rinse the beans, allow them to dry, and then reuse them.

You should store vanilla beans in a cool, dark place and preferably in an airtight container, but check them from time to time because any humidity or moisture that gets

The beans must be completely dried out before being used.

Vanilla is one of the world's most expensive spices.

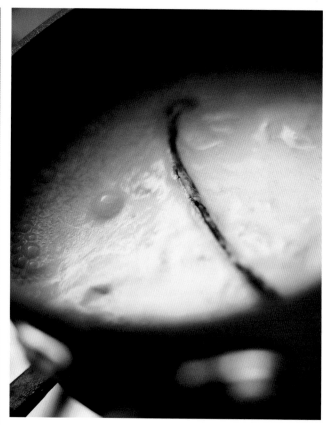

The beans can be left to dry and then reused in other recipes.

into the container is likely to make them turn moldy. In addition, if they dry out too much, the beans will become hard and unsuitable for most recipes. If they aren't too dry, it is possible to rehydrate them by steeping them in water, and they will then be perfectly fine to use.

Preparing the beans

Some recipes require whole vanilla beans, some include the seeds, and some will need both pods and seeds. To split a vanilla bean, hold it on a cutting board between your thumb and index finger, then, using a small, sharp knife, carefully draw the knife down the center of the bean, cutting through to the other side. Most of the seeds should

remain intact inside and you can then use either the tip of the knife or a small spoon to scrape them out and into whatever you're cooking. But remember, if the actual pod isn't required for the recipe, don't throw it away—it can still be put to good use.

Quick ideas

If you're not *au fait* with all things vanilla yet, you will be as soon as you start trying some of the recipes in this book. You'll find numerous ideas for cookies, cakes, and desserts, as well as a number of hot and cold drinks. From Classic Crème Caramel (see page 37) to the unusual Italian Rice Pudding (see page 14) and the mouthwatering White

Chocolate, Vanilla, and Pistachio Mousse (see page 28), there's plenty here to keep vanilla lovers contented for many meals to come.

Apart from the recipes, there are plenty of other quick ways in which you can use vanilla to add a wonderful flavor to everyday food and drinks. Here are just a few suggestions to try:

• Place a vanilla bean in your sugar jar to infuse it with a gorgeously subtle flavor that will be transferred to all your baking when you use the sugar (see page 83). When the sugar runs out, leave the vanilla bean in the container when you refill it with new sugar.

• When you make custard, add a vanilla bean and keep it in the pan as you stir. For a stronger flavor, split the bean in half and scrape the seeds into the custard while it's heating and thickening. There are also some wonderful vanilla-inspired sauces in this book: try Crème Anglaise (see page 70) or Hot Fudge Sauce (see page 81).

• Add a vanilla bean to ground coffee for a gentle hint of vanilla in freshly brewed drinks.

• For a really luxurious hot chocolate drink, gently heat the milk in a pan, adding a vanilla bean and letting it infuse. Just keep stirring and heating until the strength of the vanilla flavor is to your liking.

Vanilla extract

Many recipes call for the inclusion of vanilla extract, and this isn't always derived entirely from pure vanilla; it's often a mock flavor and aroma, or is part vanilla and part synthetic. When you buy vanilla extract, look for bottles labeled Pure Vanilla Extract. This should contain at least 35 percent alcohol, which helps to extract the flavor of the vanilla. Many brands will contain varying amounts of water and sweeteners. This is the best type of extract to buy for culinary usage.

Some recipes include vanilla bean paste, which contains (as the name suggests) vanilla bean seeds in a thick, viscous paste. Although expensive to buy, it is economical to use. It can also provide a convenient substitute for vanilla beans, with 2 teaspoons of paste being the equivalent to 1 vanilla bean.

Products labeled as Vanilla Flavoring will contain some pure vanilla, but it will be combined with vanillin, a synthetic flavor. There is also a product called Imitation Vanilla, but this is best avoided altogether because it doesn't contain any genuine vanilla flavor. Any substitute for the genuine article somewhat defeats the object of investing in a book of vanilla recipes!

It's worth paying the extra for genuine vanilla extract.

Puddings and tarts

Sticky toffee puddings

3/4 cup pitted chopped dried dates
1/2 cup unsalted butter, softened
1/2 cup superfine sugar
2 teaspoons vanilla bean paste
3 eggs
1 1/2 cups self-rising flour
1 teaspoon baking powder
cream or ice cream, to serve

Sauce
1 1/4 cups heavy cream
3/4 cup light brown sugar
1/4 cup butter

Serves 8
Preparation time 20 minutes
Cooking time 45–50 minutes

1 Put the dates in a small pan with 2/3 cup water and bring to a boil. Simmer gently for 5 minutes until the dates are soft and pulpy. Blend to a purée using an immersion blender or transfer them to a food processor and blend. Let cool.

2 Meanwhile, make the sauce. Put half the cream in a small, heavy-bottom pan with the brown sugar and butter and heat until the sugar dissolves. Bring to a boil, then let the sauce bubble for about 5 minutes until it turns to a rich, dark caramel. Stir in the remaining cream and reserve.

3 Grease 8 metal 2/3-cup pudding molds and line the bottoms with circles of waxed paper. Put the unsalted butter, superfine sugar, vanilla bean paste, eggs, flour, and baking powder in a bowl and beat with a hand-held electric beater for 1–2 minutes until pale and creamy.

4 Stir the date purée into the pudding mixture and divide it among the pudding molds. Level the tops and place the molds in a roasting pan. Pour boiling water to a depth of 3/4 inch into the pan and cover with foil. Bake the puddings in a preheated oven, 350°F, for 35–40 minutes or until they are risen and feel firm to the touch.

5 Leave the puddings in the molds while you reheat the toffee sauce, then loosen the edges of the molds and invert the puddings onto serving plates. Cover with plenty of the sauce and serve with additional cream or ice cream.

Italian rice pudding

1/3 cup raisins
3 tablespoons Marsala
1 vanilla bean
2 1/2 cups milk
2 1/2 tablespoons superfine sugar
finely grated zest of 1/2 orange, plus
   extra for decorating
1/4 teaspoon ground cinnamon
1/2 cup risotto rice
1/2 cup heavy cream
toasted slivered almonds, to decorate

Serves 3–4
Preparation time 10 minutes,
   plus infusing
Cooking time 25 minutes

1 Put the raisins and Marsala in a bowl and let stand while you make the risotto. Use the tip of a small, sharp knife to score the vanilla bean lengthwise through to the center. Put it in a medium, heavy-bottom pan with the milk, bring just to a boil, then remove from the heat and let infuse for 20 minutes.

2 Stir in the sugar, orange zest, and cinnamon and return the pan to the heat. Tip in the rice and cook very gently, stirring frequently, for about 20 minutes until the mixture is thick and creamy and the rice is tender.

3 Stir in the steeped raisins and cream and heat gently for an additional 2 minutes. Serve warm, decorated with slivered almonds and grated orange zest.

Syrupy apricot shortcake

1 1/2 cups self-rising flour
1/3 cup unsalted butter, diced
1 1/2 tablespoons superfine sugar
2 1/2 tablespoons Vanilla Sugar
  (see page 83)
1 egg
1 egg yolk
8 oz white almond paste
8–12 fresh apricots, about 1 lb, halved
  and pitted
Vanilla Syrup (see page 77), to serve

Serves 6–8
Preparation time 20 minutes
Cooking time 40 minutes

Use halved and pitted greengage or red plums instead of apricots if you prefer.

1 Grease a 9-inch loose-bottom tart pan. Put the flour in a bowl with the butter and cut in with the fingertips until the mixture resembles fine bread crumbs. Stir in the superfine sugar and 1 1/2 tablespoons of the vanilla sugar. Add the egg and egg yolk and mix to a soft dough.

2 Press the dough into the prepared pan, spreading it in an even layer using floured hands. Push the dough slightly up the sides of the pan to create a rim. Roll out the almond paste to an 8-inch circle and lay it over the center of the dough, pressing it down gently.

3 Arrange the apricots over the top of the shortcake and sprinkle with the remaining vanilla sugar. Bake in a preheated oven, 375°F, for about 40 minutes until the shortcake is turning golden and the apricots are tender. Let cool for 10 minutes, then transfer to a serving plate. Serve drizzled with plenty of Vanilla Syrup.

Hot vanilla soufflés with apricot coulis

$1/3$ cup superfine sugar, plus extra
   for dusting
$1^1/3$ cups no-soak dried apricots,
   coarsely chopped
3 tablespoons cornstarch
5 tablespoons Cointreau or other
   orange-flavored liqueur
$2/3$ cup milk
2 teaspoons vanilla bean paste
$1/2$ cup heavy cream
4 eggs, separated
confectioners' sugar, for dusting

Serves 8
Preparation time 25 minutes
Cooking time 25 minutes

For convenience, prepare the soufflés and chill them so they're all ready for last-minute cooking.

1 Grease eight $2/3$-cup ramekin dishes and dust each one lightly with superfine sugar. Put the apricots in a small pan with $1/2$ cup water and simmer gently for 3 minutes until softened. Blend $1/2$ teaspoon of the cornstarch with 1 tablespoon water and add it to the pan. Cook gently for 1 minute or until the sauce has thickened. Turn it into a food processor or blender, add the liqueur, and blend until smooth. Divide the mixture among the ramekins.

2 Blend the remaining cornstarch in a pan with a little of the milk. Add the remaining milk and heat gently, stirring, until thickened. Stir in $1/4$ cup of the superfine sugar, the vanilla bean paste, cream, and the egg yolks and turn into a large bowl.

3 Beat the egg whites until peaking and gradually beat in the remaining superfine sugar. Using a large metal spoon, fold the egg whites into the custard.

4 Spoon the mixture into the ramekins and put them on a cookie sheet. Bake in a preheated oven, 400°F, for about 20 minutes until well risen. Dust with confectioners' sugar and serve immediately.

French toast with summer fruits and cream

1¹/₂ cups strawberries

³/₄ cup redcurrants

2 cups raspberries

1 tablespoon Vanilla Sugar
   (see page 83)

squeeze of lemon juice

6 chunky slices of brioche, about
   ³/₄ inch thick

3 egg yolks

1 teaspoon vanilla extract

¹/₄ cup superfine sugar

²/₃ cup light cream

3 tablespoons milk

¹/₄ cup unsalted butter

1 tablespoon oil

whipped cream, to serve

Serves 6
Preparation time 15 minutes
Cooking time 8 minutes

Vanilla sugar and extract give a double dose of flavor to this recipe that's a perfect summer dessert.

1 Hull the strawberries and halve if they are large. Remove the redcurrants from their stalks by running them through the tines of a fork. Put all the fruits in a nonmetallic bowl and add the vanilla sugar and lemon juice. Stir lightly and let stand.

2 Meanwhile, make the French toast. Cut each slice of bread into 2 triangles. Beat together the egg yolks, vanilla extract, 1 tablespoon of the superfine sugar, the cream, and the milk.

3 Arrange the slices of bread in a single layer on 2 large plates. Pour over the egg mixture and let stand for a few minutes until it has soaked in, turning the bread once.

4 Melt the butter with the oil in a large skillet. Add half the bread slices and fry gently for 2 minutes on each side until golden. Drain and keep warm while frying the remainder.

5 Sprinkle the remaining superfine sugar on a plate and lightly turn the toast in the sugar. Serve with the fruits and spoonfuls of whipped cream.

Vanilla and banana pancakes

2 bananas
1 teaspoon vanilla extract
1 cup self-rising flour
1 teaspoon baking powder
1 tablespoon superfine sugar
1 egg
1/3 cup milk
1 tablespoon butter, melted
a little oil for frying
Vanilla Maple Butter (see page 72) or
    Hot Fudge Sauce (see page 81),
    to serve

Makes 12
Preparation time 15 minutes
Cooking time 15–20 minutes

1 Mash the bananas with the vanilla extract to make a purée. Sift the flour and baking powder into a bowl and stir in the sugar.

2 Beat the egg with the milk and melted butter and beat into the dry ingredients until smooth. Stir in the banana purée.

3 Heat a little oil in a large skillet or grill pan. Using a large metal spoon, drop in spoonfuls of the batter, spacing them well apart in the pan. (You'll probably be able to cook 3 or 4 pancakes at a time.) Cook for about 3 minutes until bubbles appear on the surface and the undersides are golden. Turn the pancakes with a spatula and cook for an additional 1–2 minutes.

4 Transfer the pancakes to a serving plate and keep them warm while cooking the remainder. Serve hot with the Vanilla Maple Butter or Hot Fudge Sauce.

Macadamia and vanilla tart

1 quantity Sweet Vanilla Pastry
  (see below)
1¹/3 cups macadamia nuts
¹/2 cup light brown sugar
²/3 cup maple syrup
¹/3 cup unsalted butter
2 teaspoons vanilla bean paste
1¹/3 cups ground almonds
4 eggs, beaten
ice cream or cream, to serve

Serves 8–10
Preparation time 30 minutes
Cooking time 45 minutes

1 Thinly roll out the pastry on a lightly floured counter and use it to line a 9-inch loose-bottom tart pan. Line the pastry with waxed paper and ceramic baking beans and bake blind in a preheated oven, 400°F, for 15 minutes. Remove the paper and beans and bake for an additional 5 minutes. Reduce the oven temperature to 325°F.

2 Coarsely chop the macadamia nuts. Put the sugar, maple syrup, and butter in a pan and heat gently until melted. Remove the pan from the heat and beat in the vanilla bean paste and ground almonds, followed by the eggs. Add half the nuts and turn the mixture into the pastry shell.

3 Sprinkle the tart with the remaining nuts and bake for about 25 minutes or until the filling forms a crust but remains quite soft underneath. Let the tart cool for 10 minutes, then serve with ice cream or cream.

Sweet vanilla pastry

1¹/4 cups all-purpose flour
¹/3 cup lightly salted butter, diced
2 tablespoons Vanilla Sugar
  (see page 83)
1 egg yolk

Makes one 8–9 inch pastry shell
Preparation time 10 minutes,
  plus chilling

1 Put the flour in a bowl with the butter and cut in with the fingertips until the mixture resembles fine bread crumbs.

2 Stir in the sugar. Add the egg yolk and 2–3 teaspoons cold water and mix to a firm dough, adding a little more water if the dough feels dry. (Alternatively, blend the butter into the flour in a food processor, then blend in the sugar, egg yolk, and water until the mixture binds together.)

3 Knead the pastry lightly on a floured surface until softened, then cover and chill for 30 minutes before using.

Toffee apple upside-down pudding

2 cooking apples, about 1 lb
1 quantity Hot Fudge Sauce
  (see page 81)
$1/2$ cup unsalted butter, softened
$1/2$ cup dark brown sugar
1 teaspoon vanilla extract
2 eggs
$1^1/4$ cups self-rising flour
$1/2$ teaspoon baking powder
Crème Anglaise (see page 70) or
  cream, to serve

Serves 6–8
Preparation time 20 minutes
Cooking time 30–35 minutes

This rich pudding should be enjoyed on cold winter days. To stop the apples from coloring once you've sliced them, drizzle over a little lemon juice.

1 Grease a shallow 9-inch cake pan and line the bottom with a circle of waxed paper. Peel and core the apples, cut them into chunky slices. Scatter them in the pan and drizzle with 6 tablespoons of the sauce.

2 Put the butter, sugar, vanilla extract, eggs, flour, and baking powder in a bowl and beat with a hand-held electric beater for 1–2 minutes until creamy. Carefully spread the mixture over the apples in the pan and level the top.

3 Bake the pudding in a preheated oven, 350°F, for 30–35 minutes or until it is firm to the touch. Let cool in the pan for 10 minutes, then invert the pudding onto a serving plate.

4 Peel away the lining paper from the pudding. Serve it warm with the remaining sauce and Crème Anglaise or cream.

Apple, blackberry, and vanilla puffs

3 cooking apples, about 1^1/$_4$ lb
^{1}/$_4$ cup plus 1 tablespoon superfine
   sugar
1^1/$_2$ teaspoons vanilla bean paste
^{1}/$_2$ teaspoon cornstarch
1 cup blackberries
1 lb puff pastry, thawed if frozen
beaten egg, to glaze
Vanilla Sugar (see page 83),
   for dusting
Crème Anglaise (see page 70), Vanilla
   Sabayon (see page 73), or cream,
   to serve

Makes 6
Preparation time 20 minutes,
   plus cooling
Cooking time 25 minutes

1 Peel and core the apples, then chop them into chunky pieces. Put the superfine sugar in a medium pan with 2 tablespoons water and the vanilla bean paste. Heat gently until the sugar dissolves. Add the apples, turning them in the syrup, cover, and simmer gently for 1 minute.

2 Blend the cornstarch with 1 tablespoon water and add it to the pan. Cook, stirring gently, until the juices have thickened. Remove the pan from the heat, turn the apple mixture into a bowl, and let cool.

3 Grease a large cookie sheet. Add the blackberries to the apple mixture and stir in lightly. Thinly roll out the pastry on a lightly floured counter and cut out 6 circles, 7^1/$_2$ inches across, using a bowl or saucer as a guide. Brush the edge of each circle with beaten egg and spoon the fruit mixture into the center.

4 Fold one side of the pastry over to meet the other and press the edges firmly together to seal. Transfer to the prepared cookie sheet. Brush the pastries with beaten egg to glaze and lightly score each one with a knife. Sprinkle the pastries with vanilla sugar and bake in a preheated oven, 400°F, for 18–20 minutes or until they are well risen and deep golden. Serve with Crème Anglaise, Vanilla Sabayon, or cream.

Steamed pudding with syrupy mango topping

1 medium mango, halved and seeded

2 tablespoons Vanilla Syrup (see page 77), plus extra for serving

$1/2$ cup unsalted butter, softened

$1/2$ cup superfine sugar

1 teaspoon vanilla extract

2 eggs

$1^1/2$ cups self-rising flour

4 tablespoons unsweetened coconut

1 tablespoon milk

Vanilla Sabayon (see page 73) or Crème Anglaise (see page 70), to serve

Serves 6
Preparation time 20 minutes
Cooking time 1 hour 40 minutes

The exotic flavors of mango, coconut, and vanilla give a new twist to the classic steamed pudding. Check the pan halfway through cooking and top up the water, if necessary.

1 Grease a 5-cup heatproof ovenproof bowl and line the bottom with a circle of waxed paper. Cut away the mango skin and cut the flesh into chunky pieces. Scatter them in the prepared bowl and drizzle with the vanilla syrup.

2 Put the butter, sugar, vanilla extract, eggs, and flour in a bowl and beat with a hand-held electric beater for 1–2 minutes until creamy. Stir in the coconut and milk and turn the mixture into the ovenproof bowl. Level the surface.

3 Cover the bowl with a double thickness of waxed paper and secure under the rim with string. Cover with foil, tucking the edges firmly under the rim.

4 Put the bowl in a steamer or large pan. Half-fill the pan with boiling water and cover with a tight-fitting lid. Steam gently for 1 hour 40 minutes, topping up the water as necessary, then let stand for 10 minutes.

5 Invert the pudding onto a serving plate and drizzle with extra vanilla syrup. Serve with Vanilla Sabayon or Crème Anglaise.

Cool desserts

White chocolate, vanilla, and pistachio mousse

1/2 cup shelled pistachio nuts
7 oz white chocolate, chopped
2/3 cup heavy cream
1 teaspoon vanilla bean paste
2/3 cup plain strained yogurt
4 egg whites
confectioners' sugar, for dusting

Serves 6
Preparation time 25 minutes,
    plus chilling
Cooking time 5 minutes

It isn't essential to skin the pistachio nuts, but they do look much prettier without the brown skins. You needn't be too thorough—just make sure you remove as many skins as you can.

1 Put the nuts in a heatproof bowl, cover with boiling water, and let stand for 1 minute. Drain well and rub between several layers of paper towels to remove the skins. Transfer the nuts to a food processor and finely chop.

2 Put the chocolate and 3 tablespoons of the cream in a medium heatproof bowl. Set over a pan of gently simmering water, making sure the bottom of the bowl doesn't come into contact with the water. Heat until melted, stirring gently once or twice until smooth.

3 Lightly whip the remaining cream with the vanilla bean paste until very lightly peaking, then stir in the yogurt. In a separate bowl, beat the egg whites until just peaking.

4 Beat the cream mixture into the melted chocolate, then fold in the egg whites. Spoon half the mousse into 6 small glass dishes or cups. Reserve some of the nuts for decoration and sprinkle the rest over the mousse. Add the remaining mousse and decorate with the reserved nuts. Chill for at least 1 hour until lightly set and serve dusted with confectioners' sugar.

Spice-infused fruit salad

1 vanilla bean
2 1/2 tablespoons superfine sugar
1 hot red chili, halved and seeded
4 clementines
2 peaches
1/2 cantaloupe melon, seeded
2/3 cup blueberries

Serves 6
Preparation time 15 minutes
Cooking time 2 minutes

The "hotness" of the syrup will depend on the type of chili you use. Go for a small, fiery one, but remove the chili from the syrup before you pour it over the fruits so the chili doesn't mask the warmth of the vanilla. Ideally, serve the fruit salad with scoops of ice cream for icy-cool contrast.

1 Use the tip of a small, sharp knife to score the vanilla bean lengthwise through to the center. Heat the sugar in a medium pan with 3/4 cup water until the sugar dissolves. Add the vanilla bean and chili and heat gently for 2 minutes. Remove the pan from the heat and let cool.

2 Cut away the zest from the clementines and slice the flesh. Pit and slice the peaches. Cut the melon flesh into small chunks, discarding the skin.

3 Mix the fruits in a serving dish and pour over the warm syrup, discarding the chili. Let the syrup cool, then cover the fruit salad and chill until you are ready to serve.

Vanilla sorbet

1/2 cup superfine sugar
1 1/3 cups dry white wine
2 teaspoons vanilla bean paste
3 tablespoons lemon juice
1 3/4 cups apple juice
4 tablespoons vodka or gin
1 egg white, lightly beaten

Serves 4–6
Preparation time 10 minutes,
   plus freezing
Cooking time 2 minutes

1 Put the sugar and wine in a medium pan and heat gently until the sugar dissolves. Remove the pan from the heat and stir in the vanilla bean paste. Let the syrup cool, then add the lemon juice, apple juice, and vodka or gin.

2 To freeze the sorbet by hand, pour the mixture into a freezer container and freeze for 4–6 hours or until it is turning mushy. Turn the sorbet into a food processor or blender and add the egg white. Blend until smooth, then return the sorbet to the freezer container and freeze for an additional 4 hours or overnight until firm.

3 To freeze the sorbet using an ice cream maker, churn the mixture until it is beginning to thicken. Add the egg white to the machine and churn again until the sorbet is firm enough to scoop. Serve the sorbet straight away or put it into a freezer container and freeze until required.

4 To serve, transfer the sorbet to the refrigerator about 30 minutes before serving if it is very solid. Serve scooped into tall glasses.

Vanilla and strawberry ripple ice cream

1 vanilla bean
1 1/3 cups milk
4 egg yolks
1/3 cup superfine sugar
1 teaspoon cornstarch
1 cup strawberries
1 tablespoon light corn syrup
1 1/3 cups heavy cream

Serves 4–6
Preparation time 20 minutes, plus
   infusing and freezing
Cooking time 5 minutes

To make plain Vanilla Ice Cream, leave out the strawberry ripple. Alternatively, to make Vanilla and Raspberry Ripple Ice Cream, use the same quantity of raspberries and add an extra spoonful of syrup if the purée tastes too sharp.

1 Use the tip of a small, sharp knife to score the vanilla bean lengthwise through to the center. Put it in a medium, heavy-bottom pan with the milk, bring just to a boil, then remove the pan from the heat and let infuse for 20 minutes.

2 Beat together the egg yolks, sugar, and cornstarch in a bowl. Remove the vanilla bean from the milk, scrape out the seeds with the tip of a knife, and return them to the milk. Pour the warm milk over the egg mixture, beating well. Return the mixture to the pan and cook over a very gentle heat for about 5 minutes, stirring constantly with a wooden spoon, until the custard has thickened. Turn the custard into a bowl, cover with a circle of waxed paper, and let cool.

3 Blend the strawberries in a food processor or blender with the corn syrup until smooth.

4 To freeze the ice cream by hand, whip the cream until lightly peaking and fold into the custard. Turn into a freezer container and freeze for 6 hours or until softly set.

5 To freeze the ice cream using an ice cream maker, stir the cream into the custard and churn the mixture until it can be softly scooped.

6 Place alternate spoonfuls of the ice cream and strawberry purée in a freezer container. Use a knife to stir through the ice cream 2 or 3 times to create a rippled effect. Don't overmix or you'll lose the contrasting flavors. Freeze the ice cream until firm.

7 To serve, transfer the ice cream to the refrigerator about 30 minutes before serving if it is very solid. Serve scooped into glasses.

Vanilla, tequila, and watermelon granita

1 vanilla bean
2/3 cup superfine sugar
4 lb watermelon
2 tablespoons lemon juice
4 tablespoons tequila

Serves 6
Preparation time 20 minutes,
    plus infusing and freezing
Cooking time 2 minutes

1 Use a small, sharp knife to score the vanilla bean lengthwise through to the center. Put it in a pan with the sugar and 2/3 cup water. Heat gently until the sugar dissolves and let the syrup infuse for 20 minutes.

2 Slice the watermelon into wedges and cut away the skin. Blend the flesh in a food processor or blender until smooth.

3 Remove the vanilla bean from the syrup, scrape out the seeds with the tip of a knife, and return them to the syrup. Beat to disperse them.

4 Strain the watermelon purée through a strainer into a freezer container and stir in the vanilla syrup, lemon juice, and tequila. Freeze for 3–4 hours until it is turning mushy. Mash with a fork and refreeze for 2–3 hours until it reaches the mushy stage again. Repeat the process once or twice more until the granita is evenly mushy. Freeze until required.

5 To serve, fork through the granita to break up the ice and pile it into tall glasses. Serve with long spoons.

Soft-centered meringues

1/3 cup light brown sugar
1 1/2 tablespoons Vanilla Sugar
  (see page 83)
1/4 cup superfine sugar
3 egg whites
1/3 cup slivered almonds

Makes about 14
Preparation time 15 minutes
Cooking time 1 hour

These soft, chewy meringues make a fabulous dessert served with whipped cream or vanilla ice cream. They're also lovely with warm fruit compotes, such as plum or apple, or with slices of fresh pineapple, melon, or bananas.

1 Line 2 cookie sheets with nonstick parchment paper. Mix together the brown, vanilla, and superfine sugars in a bowl. In a separate, thoroughly clean bowl, beat the egg whites until stiff. Gradually beat in the mixed sugars, a tablespoon at a time, beating well between each addition, until the meringue mixture is firmly peaking and glossy.

2 Use 2 dessertspoons to position spoonfuls of the meringue on the prepared cookie sheets, spacing them slightly apart. Lightly peak them with the back of a spoon and scatter with the almonds.

3 Bake the meringues in a preheated oven, 275°F, for about 1 hour until they are dry and crisp to the touch. Transfer to a cooling rack to cool.

Classic crème caramel

1 cup superfine sugar
1 vanilla bean
1 1/3 cups light cream
1 1/3 cups milk
4 eggs
4 egg yolks

Serves 6
Preparation time 20 minutes,
   plus infusing
Cooking time 45 minutes

1 Put three-quarters of the sugar in a small, heavy-bottom pan with 4 tablespoons water and heat very gently, stirring, until the sugar has dissolved. Bring to a boil and boil rapidly without stirring for 6–8 minutes until it is deep golden. Dip the bottom of the pan briefly in cold water to prevent further cooking and immediately pour the syrup into 6 ramekin dishes. While the syrup is still hot, carefully tilt each dish so the caramel comes slightly up the sides.

2 Use a small, sharp knife to score the vanilla bean lengthwise through to the center. Put it in a pan with the cream and milk, bring the mixture just to a boil, and let infuse for 20 minutes. Beat together the eggs, egg yolks, and the remaining sugar in a bowl. Remove the vanilla bean from the milk, scrape out the seeds with the tip of a knife, and return them to the milk. Pour the milk over the egg mixture, beating well.

3 Strain the mixture into a pitcher and pour it into the ramekins. Place the dishes in a roasting pan and pour enough hot water into the pan to come halfway up the sides of the ramekins. Bake the custards in a preheated oven, 300°F, for 35 minutes or until they are just firm but still have a slight wobble.

4 Remove the ramekins from the pan and let cool, then chill for several hours or overnight. To serve, loosen the edges of the custards with a sharp knife and invert them onto serving plates.

Iced vanilla parfait with cherry compote

4 egg yolks
1/2 cup granulated sugar
1 1/3 cups heavy cream
1 1/2 teaspoons vanilla bean paste

Compote
14-oz can pitted cherries in syrup
1 teaspoon cornstarch
3 tablespoons brandy

Serves 6
Preparation time 20 minutes,
 plus freezing
Cooking time 15 minutes

Use freezerproof serving dishes for the parfaits so you can serve them in the same dishes, letting them stand at room temperature for 10 minutes first if they're quite firm. Spoon a little compote over the tops or place the dishes on plates and spoon the compote around them.

1 Lightly beat the egg yolks in a large heatproof bowl. Heat a pan of water on which the bowl will rest quite snugly, but don't put the bowl over the water until you're ready to beat (see Step 3).

2 Put the sugar in a small, heavy-bottom pan with 1/2 cup water and heat gently until the sugar dissolves. Bring the syrup to a boil and boil rapidly without stirring until it registers 239°F on a candy thermometer. Alternatively, drop a teaspoonful of the syrup into a bowl of cold water and let cool for a few seconds. If it can be molded into a soft ball, the syrup is ready.

3 Using a hand-held electric beater, slowly beat the sugar syrup into the egg yolks. Set the bowl over the pan of simmering water, making sure the bottom of the bowl doesn't come into contact with the water. Beat until the mixture is thick and foamy, then remove the bowl from the heat and beat until cool.

4 Lightly whip the cream with the vanilla bean paste and fold it into the beaten mixture. Turn the parfait into 6 small freezerproof serving dishes and freeze for at least 3 hours or overnight until firm.

5 Meanwhile, make the compote. Drain the cherries, reserving the syrup. Blend the cornstarch with a little of the syrup in a small pan. Blend in the remaining syrup and cook over a moderate heat until thickened. Add the cherries and brandy and cook for an additional minute. Turn the compote into a bowl and let cool. Serve with the parfait.

Pineapple meringue tart

1 quantity Sweet Vanilla Pastry
   (see page 21)
1 medium pineapple
3 tablespoons cornstarch
2/3 cup apple juice
1/4 cup superfine sugar
3 tablespoons lemon juice
2 teaspoons vanilla extract
3 egg yolks

Meringue
3 egg whites
1/4 cup Vanilla Sugar (see page 83)
1/2 cup superfine sugar

Serves 8
Preparation time 30 minutes,
   plus cooling
Cooking time 30 minutes

1 Thinly roll out the pastry on a lightly floured counter and use it to line a 9-inch loose-bottom tart pan, 1 1/2 inches deep. Line the pastry with waxed paper and ceramic baking beans and bake blind in a preheated oven, 400°F, for 15 minutes. Remove the paper and beans and bake for an additional 5 minutes.

2 Meanwhile, cut away the skin from the pineapple. Cut it in half and remove the core and coarsely chop the flesh. Blend to a purée in a food processor or blender.

3 Blend the cornstarch with a little of the apple juice in a medium pan. Blend in the remaining apple juice and cook over a moderate heat until thickened. Stir in the sugar, lemon juice, vanilla extract, and pineapple and cook until thick and bubbling. Let the mixture cool for 5 minutes, then beat in the egg yolks. Turn the filling into the pastry shell and level the surface.

4 Make the meringue. Beat the egg whites in a thoroughly clean bowl until peaking. Gradually beat in the sugars, a tablespoon at a time, beating well between each addition, until the meringue mixture is firmly peaking and glossy. Turn out the meringue onto the filling and spread it in an even layer, peaking it attractively with a knife.

5 Bake the tart for 8–10 minutes until the meringue is pale golden. Let cool in the pan before serving.

Fresh fig and vanilla compote

12 fresh figs
1¹/3 cups port or medium sherry
¹/3 cup light brown sugar
2 teaspoons vanilla bean paste
1 tablespoon lemon juice
crème fraîche or sour cream, to serve

Serves 6
Preparation time 10 minutes,
   plus marinating
Cooking time 3 minutes

On a winter evening, this compote is just as good served warm as cold. Let the figs cool in the syrup so they fully absorb the flavor, then reheat them gently before serving.

1 Slice each fig in half, then arrange them, cut sides facing up, in a large, shallow serving dish.

2 Put the port or sherry and sugar into a pan and heat gently until the sugar dissolves. Bring the syrup to a boil and boil rapidly for 3 minutes, then remove the pan from the heat and stir in the vanilla bean paste and lemon juice.

3 Pour the hot syrup over the figs and let cool. Chill for several hours or overnight until you are ready to serve. Spoon the compote into glasses and serve with crème fraîche or sour cream.

Baked ricotta cheesecake with poached plums

2 cups ricotta cheese

1¹/₃ cups cream cheese

2 eggs

2 teaspoons vanilla bean paste

¹/₂ cup superfine sugar

Poached plums

¹/₂ small orange

1 teaspoon whole cloves

2 tablespoons dark brown sugar

1 cinnamon stick

12 oz red plums, halved and
   pitted

2 tablespoons redcurrant jelly

Serves 6

Preparation time 20 minutes

Cooking time 40 minutes

Remove the cheesecake from the pan as soon as it's thoroughly chilled. If you're making it a day in advance, let stand on the paper lining to support the cake and to stop it from drying out until you're ready to serve.

1 Lightly grease a 1-lb loaf pan and line the bottom and sides with nonstick parchment paper. Put the ricotta and cream cheese in a food processor or blender with the eggs, vanilla bean paste, and superfine sugar and blend until smooth, scraping down the mixture from the sides of the bowl.

2 Turn the mixture into the loaf pan and put it in a small roasting pan. Pour hot water into the pan to a depth of 1 inch and bake the cheesecake in a preheated oven, 325°F, for about 40 minutes until it is lightly set. Lift the cheesecake out of the water and let cool in the loaf pan.

3 Meanwhile, poach the plums. Stud the orange with the cloves and put it in a heavy-bottom pan with the brown sugar, cinnamon stick, and 3/4 cup water. Bring the water to a boil, then reduce the heat and add the plums. Cover the pan and cook the plums very gently for about 5 minutes or until they are just tender. (The cooking time will vary depending on the type of plum used.)

4 Lift out the plums and add the redcurrant jelly to the pan. Bring the liquid to a boil and boil for about 2 minutes until it is reduced and syrupy. Remove the orange and cinnamon stick and pour the syrup over the plums. Let the syrup cool, then chill the plums until you are ready to serve.

5 Remove the cheesecake from the pan and peel away the lining paper. Serve it in slices, topped with the poached plums.

Hazelnut baklava

1^{1}/$_{3}$ cups unblanched hazelnuts

^{3}/$_{4}$ cup blanched almonds

^{1}/$_{2}$ cup Vanilla Syrup (see page 77)

^{1}/$_{2}$ cup clear honey

4 teaspoons rose water or orange
   flower water

^{1}/$_{4}$ cup unsalted butter, melted

8 oz phyllo pastry, thawed if frozen

Makes 16 small squares
Preparation time 15 minutes
Cooking time 45 minutes

For best results, try to have seven or eight layers of pastry both under and over the filling. Phyllo pastry sheets come in various sizes, and if you're using very large sheets, you might need to cut them down so you have enough pastry to build up the layers.

1 Chop the hazelnuts into fairly chunky pieces. Finely chop the almonds and mix them with the hazelnuts. Mix together the vanilla syrup, honey, and rose water or orange flower water.

2 Brush a 7 x 7-inch baking pan about 1^{1}/$_{2}$ inches deep with a little of the butter and line it with a sheet of the pastry, letting the edges of the pastry overhang the sides of the pan. Brush the pastry with more butter and add another sheet of pastry. Continue to make layers until you have used half the pastry and butter. Sprinkle the nuts in an even layer over the pastry. Cover with the remaining pastry, brushing each layer with butter. Trim the excess pastry from around the edges until they are level with the top layer of pastry.

3 Bake the baklava in a preheated oven, 350°F, for about 45 minutes until it is slightly risen and golden brown. Remove the baklava from the oven and cut it into 16 small squares, making sure you cut through every layer of pastry. Pour over half the syrup and let the baklava stand until it has absorbed the syrup, then pour over the remaining syrup. Let the baklava cool completely in the pan before serving.

Florentine vanilla cheesecake

4 oz bittersweet chocolate

1/3 cup slivered almonds, lightly toasted

2 1/2 tablespoons candied citrus zest, finely chopped

6 candied cherries, finely chopped

1 cup crushed graham crackers

1/4 cup unsalted butter, melted

Filling

2 cups cream cheese

2 teaspoons vanilla bean paste

2/3 cup heavy cream

2/3 cup plain strained yogurt

1/2 cup superfine sugar

3 eggs

Serves 8–10

Preparation time 25 minutes

Cooking time 45 minutes

Leaving the cheesecake in the oven after cooking allows it to cool slowly and so prevents the surface from cracking.

1 Grease an 8-inch loose-bottom cake pan and line the sides with a strip of non-stick parchment paper. Chop half the chocolate into small pieces, reserving the remainder for decoration. Lightly crush the almonds and mix them in a bowl with the chopped chocolate, candied zest, candied cherries, crackers, and butter. Stir the mixture until well combined, then turn it into the cake pan, packing it into the bottom and slightly up the sides to form a shell.

2 Make the filling. Beat the cream cheese and vanilla bean paste in a bowl until smooth. Beat in the cream, yogurt, sugar, and eggs to make a smooth batter.

3 Pour the egg mixture into the pan and bake in a preheated oven, 325°F, for 45 minutes or until the surface feels just firm around the edges but is still very wobbly in the center. Turn off the heat and let the cheesecake cool in the oven.

4 Transfer the cheesecake to a serving plate and peel away the lining paper. Melt the remaining chocolate and use a teaspoon to drizzle the chocolate around the top edges of the cheesecake. Chill until ready to serve.

Cakes and bakes

Strawberry choux puffs

1/2 cup all-purpose flour

1/4 cup butter

2 eggs, beaten

1 teaspoon vanilla extract

2 cups strawberries, thinly sliced

1 quantity Crème Pâtissière
   (see page 76)

confectioners' sugar, for dusting

Makes 12
Preparation time 30 minutes
Cooking time 30 minutes

1 Lightly grease a large cookie sheet and sprinkle with water. Sift the flour onto a sheet of waxed paper. Cut the butter into pieces and melt it in a medium pan with 2/3 cup water. Bring the mixture to a boil, then remove the pan from the heat.

2 Tip in the flour and beat until the mixture forms a ball that comes away from the side of the pan. Let cool for 2 minutes, then gradually beat in the eggs until the mixture is smooth and glossy. Add the vanilla extract.

3 Place 12 even-size spoonfuls of the mixture, spaced well apart, on the prepared cookie sheet and bake in a preheated oven, 400°F, for about 25 minutes until they are well risen and golden. Make a slit around the middle of each and return them to the oven for 3 minutes to dry out. Transfer to a cooling rack to cool.

4 Open out each puff and divide the sliced strawberries among them. Pile the crème pâtissière on top and push the puffs back together so the strawberries and crème pâtissière still show around the center. Dust the puffs with confectioners' sugar and store them in a cool place until you are ready to serve.

Portuguese custard tarts

1 tablespoon Vanilla Sugar
   (see page 83)

1/2 teaspoon ground cinnamon

1 lb sweet short-crust pastry, thawed
   if frozen

3 eggs

2 egg yolks

2 tablespoons superfine sugar

1 teaspoon vanilla bean paste

1 1/3 cups heavy cream

2/3 cup milk

confectioners' sugar, for dusting

Makes 12
Preparation time 25 minutes
Cooking time 40 minutes

The eggs give this custard its wonderful flavor, so use the best quality ones you can buy. Like all egg custard tarts, these little tarts are best served freshly baked and with lingering warmth rather than hot or chilled.

1 Mix the vanilla sugar with the cinnamon. Cut the pastry in half and roll out each piece to an 8 x 8-inch square. Sprinkle one square with the spiced sugar and position the second square on top. Reroll the pastry to a 16 x 12-inch rectangle and cut out 12 circles, each 4 inches across, using a large cutter or small bowl as a guide.

2 Pack the pastry circles into the sections of a nonstick muffin pan, pressing them firmly into the bottom and around the sides. Line each one with a square of foil and bake blind in a preheated oven, 400°F, for 15 minutes. Remove the foil and bake for an additional 5 minutes. Reduce the oven temperature to 325°F.

3 Beat together the eggs, egg yolks, superfine sugar, and vanilla bean paste. Heat the cream and milk in a pan until it is bubbling around the edges and pour it over the egg mixture, stirring. Strain the custard into a pitcher and pour carefully into the pastry shells. Bake for about 20 minutes or until the custard is only just set. Let the tarts cool in the pan and serve dusted with confectioners' sugar.

Date cookies with vanilla maple butter

2 cups self-rising flour

1 teaspoon baking powder

$1/4$ cup unsalted butter, diced

$1/3$ cup pitted chopped dried dates

3 tablespoons superfine sugar

$1/2$ teaspoon ground allspice

1 teaspoon vanilla extract

about $2/3$ cup milk, plus extra
   for glazing

Vanilla Maple Butter (see page 72),
   to serve

Makes 10–12

Preparation time 15 minutes

Cooking time 12–15 minutes

You can use almost any other dried fruits instead of the dates. Golden raisins, prunes, apricots, figs, or blueberries are all ideal.

1 Grease a cookie sheet. Sift the flour and baking powder into a bowl. Add the butter and cut in with the fingertips until the mixture resembles fine bread crumbs. Stir in the dates, sugar, spice, and vanilla extract.

2 Add $1/2$ cup of the milk and mix to a soft dough, adding the remaining milk if the dough feels dry.

3 Turn out the dough on a floured counter and roll it out to $3/4$ inch thick. Use a cutter to cut out circles 2 inches across and transfer them to the prepared cookie sheet, rerolling the trimmings to make extra circles.

4 Brush the tops of the cookies with a little milk and bake in a preheated oven, 425°F, for 12–15 minutes until they are risen and pale golden. Transfer the cookies to a cooling rack to cool slightly and serve warm with the flavored butter.

Cranberry, orange, and vanilla muffins

1/3 cup unsalted butter, melted
3/4 cup milk
1 egg
finely grated zest of 1 orange
1 teaspoon vanilla extract
2 1/2 cups self-rising flour
2 teaspoons baking powder
2/3 cup dried cranberries
1/4 cup Vanilla Sugar (see page 83)
1/4 cup light brown sugar

Makes 12
Preparation time 10 minutes
Cooking time 15–20 minutes

Dried blueberries or cherries are equally good alternatives to the cranberries. You could also omit the orange zest and use a teaspoon of ground cinnamon or allspice instead.

1 Line a 12-section muffin pan with paper liners. Mix together the butter, milk, egg, orange zest, and vanilla extract.

2 Sift the flour and baking powder into a bowl and stir in the cranberries and the sugars.

3 Add the milk mixture to the bowl and stir briefly until only just combined. Divide the mixture among the paper liners, piling it up in the center.

4 Bake the muffins in a preheated oven, 375°F, for 15–20 minutes or until they are well risen and golden brown. Transfer them to a cooling rack to cool slightly and serve warm.

Chocolate cupcakes with vanilla butter frosting

3/4 cup unsalted butter, softened
1/2 cup superfine sugar
1 cup self-rising flour
3 eggs
1 cup ground almonds or hazelnuts
1/2 cup unblanched hazelnuts,
    coarsely chopped and toasted
3 oz white chocolate, chopped
3 oz milk chocolate, chopped

Frosting
1 cup unsalted butter, softened
1/4 cup Vanilla Sugar (see page 83)
2/3 cup confectioners' sugar
2 teaspoons lemon juice

Makes 12
Preparation time 20 minutes
Cooking time 20 minutes

1 Line a 12-section muffin pan with paper liners. Put the butter, superfine sugar, flour, eggs, and ground almonds or hazelnuts into a bowl and beat with a hand-held electric beater for 1–2 minutes until pale and creamy.

2 Reserve a handful of the chopped unblanched hazelnuts for decoration. Add the remainder to the creamed mixture with the white and milk chocolates, mix together, and divide among the paper liners.

3 Bake the cupcakes in a preheated oven, 350°F, for about 20 minutes until they are risen and just firm to the touch. Transfer to a cooling rack to cool.

4 Make the frosting. Beat together the butter, sugars, and lemon juice in a bowl until pale and fluffy. Spread the frosting over the cakes with a small spatula and decorate with the reserved nuts.

Pineapple, vanilla, and anise drizzle cake

5 whole star anise
6 tablespoons lemon juice
1 cup unsalted butter, softened
1 1/4 cups superfine sugar
2 teaspoons vanilla extract
4 eggs, beaten
2 1/2 cups self-rising flour
8 oz sweetened dried pineapple,
    coarsely chopped
1/3 cup Vanilla Sugar (see page 83)

Serves 8–10
Preparation time 20 minutes,
    plus infusing
Cooking time 1 1/4 hours

1 Grease and line the bottom and sides of a cake pan, either 7 x 7-inches square or 8-inches round. Put the star anise, lemon juice, and 3 tablespoons water in a small pan, cover, and heat gently for 3 minutes. Remove from the heat and let infuse while you make the cake.

2 Beat together the butter, 1 cup of the superfine sugar, and the vanilla extract until pale and fluffy. Gradually beat in the eggs, a little at a time, adding a little of the flour if the mixture starts to curdle. Sift the remaining flour into the bowl and fold it in using a large metal spoon. Stir in two-thirds of the pineapple and turn the mixture into the prepared pan. Level the top and sprinkle with the remaining pineapple.

3 Bake the cake in a preheated oven, 325°F, for about 1 1/4 hours or until it is risen and firm to the touch.

4 Add the vanilla sugar and the remaining superfine sugar to the lemon and anise in the pan and drizzle the syrup over the cake while it is still warm.

Sugared angel cake

8 egg whites

1 teaspoon cream of tartar

1 1/2 teaspoons vanilla bean paste

1 teaspoon finely grated lemon zest

1 cup superfine sugar

1 1/2 cups all-purpose flour, plus extra
   for dusting

Vanilla Sugar (see page 83),
   for dusting

fresh raspberries, to decorate

whipped cream, to serve

Serves 12
Preparation time 20 minutes
Cooking time 30–35 minutes

Angel cake is lovely served with a cup of coffee or tea or as a dessert with a bowl of soft fruits. Alternatively, lightly whip 1 cup heavy cream with 1/2 teaspoon vanilla bean paste and swirl it over the cake. Serve decorated with raspberries.

1 Brush a 7-cup tube pan with oil and coat with flour, shaking off the excess. Beat the egg whites in a large, thoroughly clean bowl until frothy. Add the cream of tartar and beat again until the egg whites are softly peaking. Beat in the vanilla bean paste and the lemon zest.

2 Gradually beat in the superfine sugar, a tablespoon at a time, beating well between each addition, until the mixture is glossy. Sift the flour over the mixture and gently fold it in using a large metal spoon. Turn the mixture into the prepared pan and level the surface.

3 Bake the cake in a preheated oven, 325°F, for 30–35 minutes or until it is firm to the touch and a skewer inserted into the center comes out clean.

4 Invert the pan onto a cooling rack and let the cake cool upside down. When the cake is completely cold, loosen the edges with a knife and turn it out onto a serving plate.

5 Generously dust the cake with vanilla sugar and surround with raspberries to decorate. Serve with whipped cream.

Marbled espresso and vanilla cake

1 tablespoon instant espresso coffee
3/4 cup unsalted butter, softened
3/4 cup superfine sugar
3 eggs
1 3/4 cups self-rising flour
1/2 teaspoon baking powder
1 teaspoon vanilla extract
Vanilla Maple Butter (see page 72)
unsweetened cocoa powder,
    for dusting

Serves 8–10
Preparation time 20 minutes
Cooking time 50 minutes

1 Grease and line the bottom of a 7 1/2-inch loose-bottom cake pan or springform pan. Mix the coffee with 1 tablespoon hot water.

2 Put the butter, sugar, eggs, flour, and baking powder in a bowl and beat with a hand-held electric beater for 1–2 minutes until pale and creamy. Spoon half the mixture into a separate bowl. Add the vanilla extract to one bowl and the coffee to the other.

3 Place heaped teaspoonfuls of the coffee mixture in the prepared pan, spacing them well apart and using about half the mixture. Spoon about half the vanilla mixture into the gaps over the base of the pan. Layer with the remaining mixtures, keeping the flavors separate if possible, then level the surface. Lightly swirl a knife through the mixtures to marble them together. Don't overmix, or the colors and flavors will merge.

4 Bake the cake in a preheated oven, 350°F, for about 50 minutes or until it is firm to the touch. Transfer to a cooling rack to cool.

5 Swirl the top of the cake with the Vanilla Maple Butter and serve dusted with a little cocoa.

Blueberry and vanilla loaf cake

1/2 cup unsalted butter, softened
1/2 cup superfine sugar
2 eggs
1 1/4 cups self-rising flour
1/2 teaspoon baking powder
2/3 cup ground almonds
2 teaspoons vanilla extract
1 1/3 cups blueberries
Vanilla Sugar (see page 83),
    for dusting

Serves 8
Preparation time 15 minutes
Cooking time 40–45 minutes

1 Grease and line the bottom and sides of a 1-lb loaf pan with a double thickness of waxed paper, making sure the paper comes 1 inch above the rim to allow for rising.

2 Put the butter, superfine sugar, eggs, flour, baking powder, ground almonds, and vanilla extract in a bowl and beat with a hand-held electric beater for 1–2 minutes until pale and creamy. Fold in two-thirds of the blueberries and turn the mixture into the prepared pan. Level the top and sprinkle with the remaining blueberries.

3 Bake the cake in a preheated oven, 350°F, for 40–45 minutes until it is well risen and firm to the touch. Let cool in the pan for 10 minutes.

4 Turn out the cake onto a cooling rack and sprinkle the top generously with vanilla sugar. Transfer to a serving plate.

Vanilla biscotti

1/2 cup whole unblanched almonds
1/4 cup unsalted butter, softened
1/2 cup superfine sugar
1 1/2 cups self-rising flour
1 1/2 teaspoons baking powder
1 teaspoon ground coriander
2/3 cup ground almonds
2 eggs
finely grated zest of 1 lemon
2 teaspoons vanilla extract
confectioners' sugar, for dusting

Makes 24
Preparation time 15 minutes,
    plus cooling
Cooking time 40 minutes

1 Grease a large cookie sheet. Spread the almonds out on a separate dry cookie sheet and lightly toast under a medium broiler for 1–2 minutes. Let the almonds cool, then coarsely chop.

2 Cream together the butter and superfine sugar in a bowl. Sift the flour, baking powder, and coriander into the bowl. Stir in the ground and the toasted chopped almonds. Beat together the eggs, lemon zest, and vanilla extract and add the mixture to the bowl. Mix to a soft dough.

3 Turn out the dough on a lightly floured counter and cut it in half. Shape each piece into a log about 9 inches long. Transfer the 2 pieces to the prepared cookie sheet, spacing them well apart, and flatten each one to about 1/2 inch.

4 Bake the logs in a preheated oven, 325°F, for about 30 minutes until they are risen and just firm. Let cool, then cut each log across into about 12 thin slices. Return the slices to the oven and bake for an additional 10 minutes to crisp them up. Transfer the biscotti to a cooling rack to cool and serve dusted with confectioners' sugar.

Chocolate chip vanilla cookies

1/2 cup unsalted butter, softened
1/4 cup superfine sugar
1/4 cup Vanilla Sugar (see page 83)
1 egg
1 1/4 cups porridge oats
1 1/4 cups self-rising flour
8 oz milk chocolate, chopped

Makes 18–20
Preparation time 15 minutes
Cooking time 15–20 minutes

Instead of milk chocolate, you could use bittersweet or white chocolate, or a mixture of the different flavors.

1 Grease a large cookie sheet. Use a hand-held electric beater to beat together the butter and sugars in a bowl until pale and creamy. Beat in the egg, then add the oats and flour and stir until combined. Stir in the chocolate.

2 Place heaped dessertspoonfuls of the mixture on the prepared cookie sheet, spacing them well apart, and flatten each one slightly with the back of a fork.

3 Bake the cookies in a preheated oven, 350°F, for 15–20 minutes until they are risen and pale golden. Let stand on the cookie sheet for 5 minutes to firm up slightly, then transfer them to a cooling rack to cool.

Vanilla fudge cookies

6 oz vanilla fudge
1³/₄ cups self-rising flour
1 teaspoon baking powder
¹/₂ cup unsalted butter, diced
¹/₃ cup light brown sugar
1 egg
1 teaspoon vanilla extract
Vanilla Sugar (see page 83),
    for dusting

Makes 16
Preparation time 15 minutes,
    plus chilling
Cooking time 20 minutes

1 Grease a large cookie sheet. Chop the fudge into small pieces and set aside. Put the flour and baking powder in a bowl with the butter and cut in with the fingertips until the mixture resembles fine bread crumbs. Stir in the brown sugar.

2 Beat the egg with the vanilla extract and add the mixture to the bowl. Use your hands to mix it to a dough and turn it out onto a lightly floured counter. Shape the dough into a log about 8 inches long and wrap it in waxed paper. Chill for at least 1 hour.

3 Cut the log across into 16 thick slices and place them, spaced well apart, on the prepared cookie sheet. Bake in a preheated oven, 350°F, for about 15 minutes. Remove the cookies from the oven and sprinkle with the chopped fudge, pressing the pieces of fudge firmly into the dough. Return the cookies to the oven for an additional 5 minutes or until they are turning golden. Take care that the fudge does not melt over the edges of the cookies.

4 Let the cookies stand on the cookie sheet for 2 minutes, then transfer them to a cooling rack. Let cool and serve dusted with vanilla sugar.

Baby macaroons

2 egg whites
$1/2$ cup superfine sugar
1 teaspoon vanilla bean paste
$1^1/3$ cups ground almonds
$2/3$ cup unsweetened coconut
about 24 whole unblanched almonds

Makes about 24
Preparation time 10 minutes
Cooking time 20 minutes

1 Line a large cookie sheet with nonstick parchment paper. Beat the egg whites until peaking, then gradually beat in the sugar, a tablespoon at a time, until the mixture is thick and glossy. Add the vanilla bean paste with the last of the sugar.

2 Gently fold in the ground almonds and coconut with a large metal spoon until evenly combined.

3 Use 2 teaspoons to place spoonfuls of the mixture, spaced slightly apart, on the prepared cookie sheet. Press a whole almond on the top of each macaroon and bake in a preheated oven, 350°F, for 20 minutes until they are pale golden and just firm to the touch. Let the macaroons cool on the cookie sheet.

Sugar, sauces, and frostings

Crème anglaise

1 vanilla bean
3 bay leaves or 3 rosemary sprigs
1$\frac{1}{3}$ cups milk
1$\frac{1}{3}$ cups light cream
6 egg yolks
2 tablespoons superfine sugar

Serves 6
Preparation time 10 minutes,
    plus infusing
Cooking time 15 minutes

Don't be tempted to cook the custard over a high setting or it might curdle. The bay leaves or rosemary sprigs are not essential, but they do provide a delicious flavor that complements the vanilla.

1 Use the tip of a small, sharp knife to score the vanilla bean lengthwise through to the center. Put it in a heavy-bottom pan with the bay leaves or rosemary, milk, and cream and bring the mixture slowly to a boil. Remove the pan from the heat and let infuse for 20 minutes.

2 Beat together the egg yolks and sugar in a bowl. Remove the herb and vanilla bean from the milk, scrape out the seeds of the vanilla bean with the tip of a knife, and return them to the milk.

3 Pour the milk over the eggs and sugar, beating well. Return the mixture to the cleaned pan and cook over a very gentle heat, stirring constantly with a wooden spoon, until the sauce is thick enough to coat the back of the spoon. This might take up to 10 minutes. Pour the sauce into a pitcher and serve warm.

Vanilla maple butter

1/2 cup unsalted butter, softened
1 1/2 teaspoons vanilla bean paste
2 tablespoons confectioners' sugar
1/2 cup pure maple syrup

Makes 7 oz
Preparation time 5 minutes

This silky smooth butter makes an irresistible topping or filling for sponge cakes. It's also delicious spread over warm bread, muffins, and cupcakes, or melted over pancakes and baked bananas.

1 Put the butter, vanilla bean paste, and sugar in a small bowl and beat with a hand-held electric beater until the ingredients are combined.

2 Gradually blend in the maple syrup, a little at a time, until the mixture is soft and smooth. Transfer the butter to a small serving dish, cover, and chill until required. The butter can be kept in the refrigerator for up to 1 week.

Vanilla sabayon

4 egg yolks
2 tablespoons Vanilla Sugar
   (see page 83)
1 teaspoon vanilla extract
2 tablespoons Marsala

Serves 3–4
Preparation time 5–8 minutes,
   plus standing
Cooking time 5 minutes

Served warm or cold, sabayon sauce makes a lovely summer dessert when it is spooned over a salad of soft fruits or a freshly baked fruit pie. Alternatively, pour it into small glasses and serve with dessert cookies.

1 Blend the egg yolks, vanilla sugar, vanilla extract, and Marsala in a large heatproof bowl. Set the bowl over a pan of gently simmering water, making sure the bottom of the bowl doesn't come into contact with the water.

2 Use a hand-held electric beater or balloon whisk to beat the mixture for about 5 minutes until it is light and aerated and the beater leaves a trail when lifted from the bowl.

3 If you are serving the sauce hot, use it immediately. If it is to be served cold, remove the bowl from the heat and beat for an additional 2–3 minutes until it is cool. Let the sauce stand for up to 10 minutes before serving.

Vanilla and strawberry coulis

2 cups strawberries
1 teaspoon vanilla bean paste
2 tablespoons confectioners' sugar
2 teaspoons lemon juice

Serves 6
Preparation time 5 minutes

Make sure you use really well-flavored, fragrant strawberries for this sauce, otherwise it will be thin-flavored and watery. Like all coulis, this makes a perfect accompaniment to hot and cold desserts, including cheesecakes, white and dark chocolate dishes, and pancakes.

1 Hull the strawberries and put them in a food processor or blender with the vanilla bean paste, sugar, and lemon juice.

2 Blend the strawberries to a smooth sauce, scraping down any pieces of fruit from the sides of the bowl. Pour the coulis into a pitcher, cover, and chill until required. The coulis can be kept in the refrigerator for up to 3 days.

Crème pâtissière

2/3 cup milk
2/3 cup heavy cream
1 vanilla bean
4 egg yolks
3 tablespoons superfine sugar
2 tablespoons all-purpose flour

Serves 4–6
Preparation time 10 minutes,
   plus infusing
Cooking time 5 minutes

Use this thick, creamy custard as a filling for a pastry or sponge shell, piling it with soft fruits to make a fabulous summer dessert. Alternatively, pack it into choux buns or profiteroles instead of whipped cream (see page 48). The quantities can easily be doubled.

1 Put the milk and cream into a medium, heavy-bottom pan. Use the tip of a small, sharp knife to score the vanilla bean lengthwise through to the center. Add it to the pan and bring the mixture to a boil. Remove the pan from the heat and let infuse for 20 minutes.

2 Beat together the egg yolks, sugar, and flour until smooth. Remove the vanilla bean from the milk, scrape out the seeds with the tip of a knife, and return them to the milk. Pour the milk over the egg mixture, beating well.

3 Return the custard to the pan and cook over a gentle heat, stirring constantly with a wooden spoon, for 4–5 minutes until it is thick and smooth. Turn the custard into a small bowl and cover with waxed paper to prevent a skin from forming. Let cool before use.

Homemade vanilla syrup

3/4 cup superfine sugar
2 vanilla beans

Makes 3/4 cup
Preparation time 5 minutes
Cooking time 8 minutes

Homemade vanilla syrup makes a great gift. Pour it into small bottles and immerse a fresh bean in the syrup. Try adding a couple of cinnamon sticks or a spoonful of whole cloves with the vanilla, or add a splash of vodka or brandy to the cooled syrup. Vanilla syrup is a perfect topping for pancakes, waffles, or ice cream and is delicious stirred into fruit compotes.

1 Put the sugar into a small, heavy-bottom pan with 1/2 cup water and heat very gently, stirring, until the sugar dissolves. Bring to a boil and boil rapidly, without stirring, for 6–8 minutes until the syrup is deep golden. Immediately dip the bottom of the pan into cold water to prevent further cooking. Stir in another 1/2 cup water.

2 Use a small, sharp knife to score each vanilla bean lengthwise through to the center. Add them to the syrup and return to the heat. Cook gently, stirring, until the caramel is smooth.

3 Let the syrup cool completely. Transfer the syrup and the vanilla beans to a thoroughly clean bottle and let stand for several days before use, shaking the bottle frequently.

Blueberry and apple conserve

2–3 cooking apples, about 1 lb, peeled,
   cored, and cut into small chunks
1/3 cup superfine sugar
1 teaspoon cornstarch
1 tablespoon lemon juice
1 cup blueberries
2 teaspoons vanilla bean paste

Makes 1 lb
Preparation time 15 minutes
Cooking time 5 minutes

Tangy and refreshing, this conserve is a delicious change from more traditional preserves on toast, waffles, or pancakes. If you prefer a sweeter flavor, add an additional 2 tablespoons sugar.

1 Put the apples, sugar, and 4 tablespoons water in a medium, heavy-bottom pan. Cover and heat gently for 3–5 minutes until the apples are tender but not falling apart. (Check frequently during cooking because the cooking time will vary depending on the type of apple used.)

2 Blend the cornstarch with 2 tablespoons water in a small bowl and add it to the pan with the lemon juice. Heat gently, stirring constantly, until the mixture is slightly thickened.

3 Remove the pan from the heat and stir in the blueberries and vanilla bean paste. Transfer the conserve to a bowl or jar and let cool completely. It can be stored in the refrigerator for up to a week.

Vanilla and ricotta frosting

2/3 cup heavy cream

finely grated zest of 1 lime, plus
  2 teaspoons juice

1 1/2 teaspoons vanilla bean paste

3/4 cup confectioners' sugar

1 cup ricotta cheese

Makes about 2 cups
Preparation time 5 minutes

This is the perfect recipe for anyone who doesn't like really sugary frostings. Smooth and creamy, you can afford to smooth it generously over buttery sponge cakes, cupcakes, light fruit cakes, or carrot cake.

1 Put the cream, lime zest and juice, vanilla bean paste, and sugar in a bowl and beat with a hand-held electric beater until firmly peaking.

2 Stir the ricotta cheese to break it up, then add it to the bowl. Stir well until evenly combined.

Hot fudge sauce

1/3 cup unsalted butter, diced
3/4 cup light brown sugar
6-oz can evaporated milk
2 teaspoons vanilla extract

Serves 6
Preparation time 5 minutes
Cooking time 5 minutes

This buttery fudge sauce can easily be made ahead and reheated if you don't fancy last-minute cooking. It makes a delicious treat over warm fruit or nut muffins, baked bananas, ice cream, or steamed puddings, or even swirled into thick yogurt.

1 Put the butter and sugar in a small, heavy-bottom pan. Heat very gently, stirring with a wooden spoon, until the butter has melted and the sugar has dissolved. Bring the mixture to a boil and boil for about 2 minutes or until the syrup has the consistency of molasses. Remove the pan from the heat.

2 Stir in the evaporated milk and vanilla extract and return the mixture to the heat. Bring to a boil and boil for about a minute until the sauce is smooth and glossy. Transfer to a pitcher and serve warm.

Homemade vanilla sugar

2 vanilla beans
1 cup superfine sugar

Makes 1 cup
Preparation time 2 minutes

Vanilla sugar can be stored for several weeks before it's used, by which time it'll be well flavored and aromatic. As you use the sugar, top up the jar with fresh sugar for an ongoing supply until the vanilla loses its strength. Substitute 2–4 tablespoons vanilla sugar for ordinary sugar in recipes for puddings, desserts, sauces, cakes, and cookies, or use it to sprinkle over doughnuts and waffles.

1 Use a small, sharp knife to cut each vanilla bean in half lengthwise, then cut each length in half to make 8 pieces.

2 Put the sugar in a glass jar and push the vanilla pieces into it. Cover with a lid and store for about a week before using, shaking the jar occasionally to disperse the vanilla flavor.

Drinks

Vanilla-infused tea

1 wedge clementine or mandarin
1 wedge grapefruit
1 lemon thyme sprig
1/2 vanilla bean
1/2 teaspoon honey (optional)

Makes 1 cup
Preparation time 2–3 minutes

Mixed with tangy citrus fruits, an aromatic vanilla bean makes a delicious and comforting herbal tea. The flavors are so pronounced that you can top up the glass with boiling water several times before it loses its refreshing taste, giving you a supply of healthy drinks through the day. Try other citrus fruits, such as lime, lemon, or orange, and other herbs, such as bay leaves, rosemary, or lemon balm.

1 Put the citrus fruit and thyme in a heatproof glass or cup. Use a small, sharp knife to score the vanilla bean through to the center. Add it to the glass or cup with the honey, if using.

2 Top up the glass or cup with boiling water and let infuse for 2–3 minutes, stirring gently, before serving.

Hot vanilla

1¾ cups milk
4 oz good-quality white chocolate,
  chopped
1 teaspoon vanilla bean paste
unsweetened cocoa, for sprinkling
vanilla beans, to decorate (optional)

Makes 2 mugs
Preparation time 5 minutes,
  plus standing
Cooking time 2 minutes

This is a perfect drink for people who like the sweetness of white chocolate.
For a less sweet version, use milk or bittersweet chocolate instead of white.

1 Pour the milk into a pan and bring it almost to a boil. Remove it from the heat
and tip in the chocolate. Let stand for 2–3 minutes, stirring frequently, until the
chocolate has melted.

2 Add the vanilla bean paste to the pan. Beat with a balloon whisk or an immersion
blender until the milk is smooth and topped with a thick foam.

3 Divide the hot vanilla between 2 mugs and serve sprinkled with cocoa. Decorate
with vanilla beans, if you like.

Iced vanilla coffee

2/3 cup very strong espresso coffee, chilled
1 1/3 cups milk
1 teaspoon vanilla extract
2 large scoops vanilla ice cream
1/2 cup whipping cream
several chocolate-coated coffee beans, crushed

Makes 2 glasses
Preparation time 5 minutes

For a mocha version, heat half the milk in a small pan and stir in 2 oz chopped bittersweet chocolate until it melts. Let cool, then stir in the remaining milk and finish as described below.

1 Pour the coffee and milk into a food processor or blender and add the vanilla extract and ice cream. Blend until smooth and frothy and pour into 2 tall glasses.

2 Lightly whip the cream and spoon it over the coffee. Sprinkle with crushed chocolate-coated coffee beans to serve.

Creamy vanilla sodas

4 passion fruit
6 scoops vanilla ice cream
5 tablespoons Vanilla Syrup (see page 77)
2/3–1 cup soda water

Makes 2 glasses
Preparation time 5 minutes

The passion fruit give this summery drink a sweet, fragrant tang. If you can't get hold of passion fruit, add a splash of freshly squeezed orange, mango, or pineapple juice.

1 Halve the passion fruit and scoop the pulp into a food processor or blender. Add 4 scoops of ice cream and the vanilla syrup. Blend until smooth.

2 Pour into 2 glasses and top up with soda water. Add another scoop of ice cream to each glass and serve at once, with stirrers.

Marbled peach milkshake

1 1/4 cups raspberries
4 teaspoons honey
2 large juicy peaches, pitted
1 teaspoon vanilla bean paste
1/2 cup light cream
2/3 cup freshly squeezed orange juice

Makes 2 glasses
Preparation time 10 minutes

1 Blend the raspberries in a food processor or blender to make a smooth purée. Press through a nonmetallic strainer to remove the seeds and stir in half the honey. Check the sweetness, adding a little extra honey, if you like.

2 Coarsely chop the peaches. Rinse out the food processor or blender and blend the peaches to a purée with the vanilla bean paste and cream, scraping any pieces down from the sides of the bowl if necessary. Blend in the orange juice and the remaining honey.

3 Use a small ladle or spoon to put peach mixture to the depth of about 3/4 inch in 2 glasses. Spoon a layer of raspberry purée on top and repeat the layering. Lightly marble the 2 colors together with a knife and serve.

Vanilla yogurt smoothie

3/4 cup plain yogurt
1 teaspoon vanilla bean paste
2 tablespoons honey
1 1/3 cups freshly pressed apple juice

Makes 2 glasses
Preparation time 3 minutes

For an extra frothy top, pour into a pitcher and blend briefly with an immersion blender. To make sure it's served thoroughly chilled, use all ingredients straight from the refrigerator or pour the smoothie over ice cubes in tall glasses.

1 Put the yogurt, vanilla bean paste, and honey in a food processor or blender and blend until evenly combined.

2 With the machine running, gradually add the apple juice until the mixture is foamy on the top. Pour into glasses and serve immediately.

Summer fruit slush

2^1/$_2$–3 cups summer fruits (e.g.,
  strawberries, raspberries,
  redcurrants, or blackberries),
  about 12 oz
about 5 tablespoons Vanilla Syrup (see
  page 77), plus extra to serve
plenty of crushed ice
extra fruits, to decorate

Makes 2 glasses
Preparation time 5 minutes

The vanilla-flavored fruit syrup should be sweet and have an intense taste before it's poured over the ice because the flavor will be diluted as the ice melts. Use really ripe, well-flavored seasonal fruits for the best results.

1 Hull the strawberries and blend the fruit in a food processor or blender until completely smooth. Strain the purée through a nonmetallic strainer into a pitcher to remove the seeds. Stir in the vanilla syrup.

2 Fill 2 tall, narrow drinking glasses or sundae glasses with crushed ice and pour in the vanilla-flavored fruit juice.

3 Pile extra fruits on top of the glasses. Serve with long spoons and extra syrup, if you like, for stirring in.

Spicy vanilla cordial

^{1}/$_3$ cup light brown sugar
^{1}/$_4$ cup Vanilla Sugar (see page 83)
finely grated zest and juice of 1 lemon
1 teaspoon grated fresh gingerroot
ice cubes and sparkling water, to serve

Makes ^{2}/$_3$ **cup**
Preparation time 5 minutes
Cooking time 5 minutes

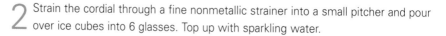

This recipe makes enough cordial for 6 glasses, but the quantities can be easily doubled. You can make the cordial ahead; it can be stored in a small, thoroughly clean bottle in the refrigerator for up to 2 weeks.

1 Put the brown sugar in a small, heavy-bottom pan with ^{1}/$_2$ cup water. Heat gently until the sugar dissolves, then bring the syrup to a boil and boil for 3 minutes. Remove the pan from the heat, add the vanilla sugar, lemon zest and juice, and ginger, and stir until the sugar dissolves. Let cool.

2 Strain the cordial through a fine nonmetallic strainer into a small pitcher and pour over ice cubes into 6 glasses. Top up with sparkling water.

index

acknowledgments

Food Stylist: Joanna Farrow
Photography: Gareth Sambidge